COLOR ME GENESIS

Stories from The Book of Genesis for Kids

In the beginning, God created the heavens and the earth, all by Himself. God is the Alpha and the Omega. He doesn't need any help.

NLT (Genesis 1:1 In the beginning God created the heavens and the earth.)

**God created the sun, the moon, the day and night.
He said, "Let there be light." And there was light!**

NLT (Genesis 1:3 And God said, "Let there be light," and there was light.)

God created the sea, the land, the grass, and the trees.
He also created the animals, the birds, and the bees.

NKJ (Genesis 1:11 Then God said, "Let the earth bring forth grass, the herb that yields seed, and the fruit tree that yields fruit according to its kind, whose seed is in itself, on the earth"; and it was so.)

Next, He created man. God gave him the breath of life, and the man started to breathe. He named this man Adam. And from his rib, God gave him a helpmate named Eve.

NIV (Genesis 2:7 And the Lord God formed man of the dust of the ground, and breathed into his nostrils the breath of life; and man became a living being.)

Adam and Eve lived in a garden called Eden. It was filled with animals, fruit, and leaves.

One day Eve was tricked by a Serpent into disobeying God. Eve was deceived.

NKJV Gen 3:4 Then the serpent said to the woman, "You will not surely die."

As a result of disobedience, Adam and Eve had to leave Eden and find a new home. Soon after, they had children. That's when Cain and Abel came along.

ESV (Genesis 3:23 Therefore the Lord God sent him out of the garden of Eden to till the ground from which he was taken.)

Cain and Abel gave offerings to God. Abel's offering was pleasing in God's eyes. Cain became very angry. So, he planned his brother's demise.

NKJV (Genesis 4:4-5 Abel also brought of the firstborn of his flock and of their fat. And the Lord respected Abel and his offering, 5v but He did not respect Cain and his offering. And Cain was very angry, and his countenance fell.)

Cain killed Abel in a field, leaving God very displeased. As punishment, God banished Cain from the land. Cain had to leave.

KJV (Genesis 4:8 Now Cain talked with Abel his brother; and it came to pass, when they were in the field, that Cain rose up against Abel his brother and killed him.)

Genesis also tells us a story of about a man named Noah. He was a very righteous man. He was chosen to build an ark. God was sending a flood to destroy the land.

NKJV (Genesis 6:9 This is the genealogy of Noah. Noah was a just man, perfect in his generations. Noah walked with God.)

Noah was ordered to
take a pair of each living
thing into the ark with
him and his family.

He also warned others
about the flood, but they
laughed at him and
called him crazy.

ESV (Genesis 6:13 And God said to Noah, "The
end of all flesh has come before Me, for the
earth is filled with violence through them; and
behold, I will destroy them with the earth")

Then one day, just as Noah said, God sent a flood. It washed everyone and everything away.
Only those on the ark with Noah were spared. The creatures, Noah, and his family were okay.

JUB (Genesis 7:7 So Noah, with his sons, his wife, and his sons' wives, went into the ark because of the waters of the flood.)

For forty days and forty nights, rain poured endlessly from the sky. Once the rain stopped, Noah sent out a Raven and then a dove to see if the land was dry.

NKJV (Genesis 7:17 Now the flood was on the earth forty days. The waters increased and lifted up the ark, and it rose high above the earth.)

Finally, the dove returned with an olive leaf.
Hooray! The flood was gone. Noah was spared because of his belief.

NKJV (Genesis: 8:11 Then the dove came to him in the evening, and behold, a freshly plucked olive leaf was in her mouth; and Noah knew that the waters had receded from the earth.)

God made Noah a promise to never destroy the world with a flood again. He sent a rainbow as a symbol of his covenant with Noah and of his promise to man.

NKJV (Genesis 9:13 I set my rainbow in the cloud, and it shall be for the sign of the covenant between Me and the earth.)

In the book of Genesis,
there's a story about the
Tower of Babel. This story is
very unique.
In the beginning, the world
only had one language and
one speech.

NKJV (Genesis 11:1 Now the whole earth
had one language and one speech.)

Noah's descendants settled in Babylon, in the land of Shinar, and the land was good.
They started to build the city using bricks and stones.
They built as much as they could.

NKJV (Genesis 11:2 And it came to pass, as they journeyed from the east, that they found a plain in the land of Shinar, and they dwelt there.)

One day, they decided to build a tower that would reach the heavens. They wanted to be like God. They thought they didn't need Him anymore.

God didn't like the pride and arrogance of the people. So, He did something He had never done before.

NKJV (Genesis: 11:6 And the Lord said, "Indeed the people are one and they all have one language, and this is what they begin to do; now nothing that they propose to do will be withheld from them.")

God confused the people by giving them different languages.
He gave them different speech and tongues. They could no longer understand each other.
The tower was full of babble and
confusion wasn't fun.

ESV (Genesis 11:7 "Come, let Us go down and there confuse their language, that they may not understand one another's speech.")

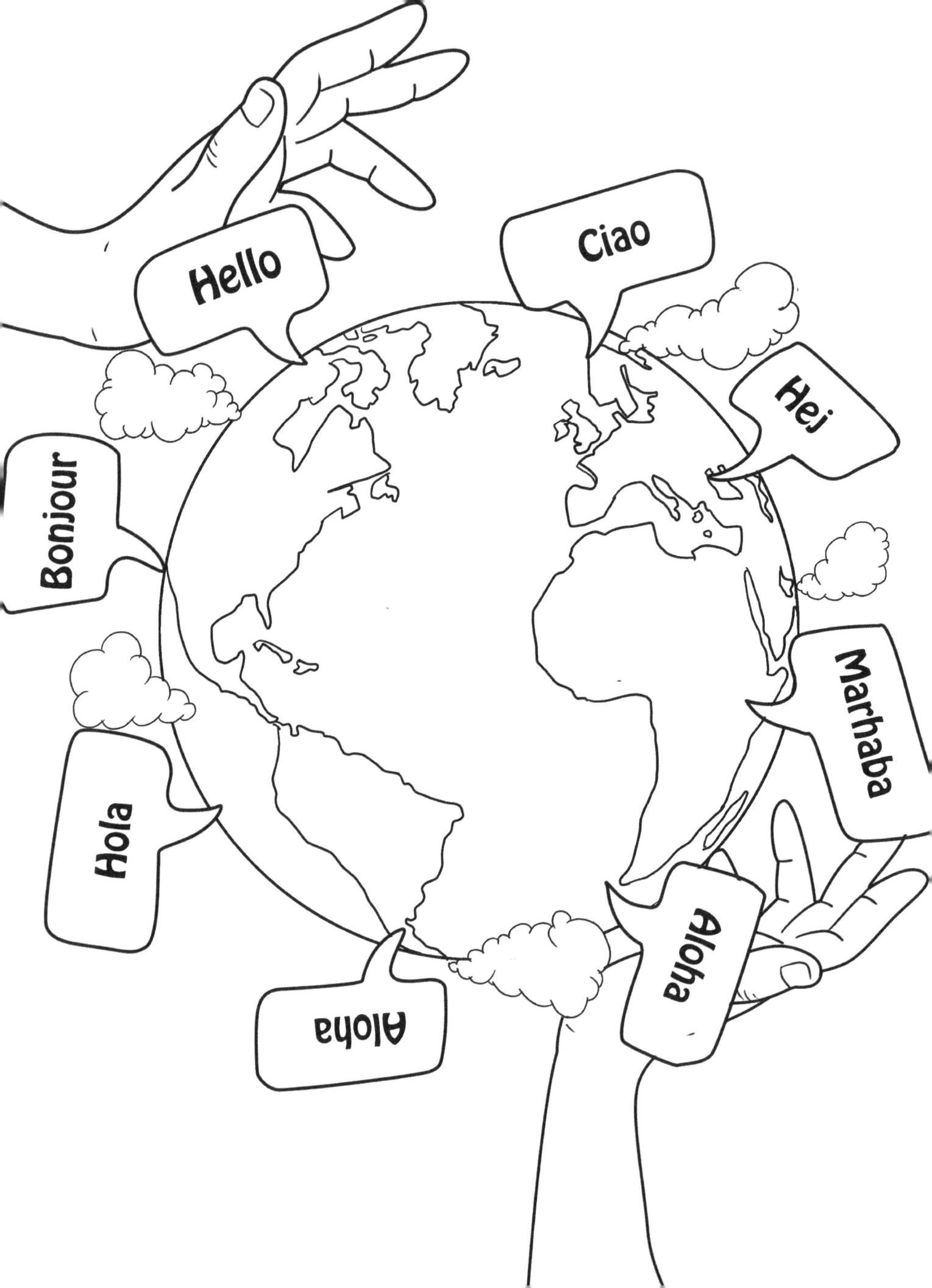

The people were scattered all over the earth, speaking different languages, just like today. God makes no mistakes. His plan is perfect in every way.

NKJV (Genesis: 11:8 So the Lord scattered them abroad from there over the face of all the earth, and they ceased building the city.)

The Book of Genesis

Genesis is the first book of the Bible. Revelations is the last. Genesis teaches us
lessons, and it teaches us about the past.

The book of Genesis tells
us where we came from,
and how things came to
be.
The book of Genesis is a
part of you, and it's a
part
of me.

This easy-to-understand book is the perfect introduction to the Bible for children. The book of Genesis touches on four important stories: The Creation Story, Cain and Abel, Noah's Ark, and the Tower of Babel.

COLOR ME GENESIS

Stories from The Book of Genesis for Kids

www.ingramcontent.com/pod-product-compliance
Lightning Source LLC
LaVergne TN
LVHW061330060426
835513LV00015B/1351